T0166042

A Fox Dreaming

Brian David Granatir

iUniverse, Inc.
New York Bloomington

A Fox Dreaming
A Collection Of Poems

iUniverse books may be ordered through booksellers or by contacting:

iUniverse
1663 Liberty Drive
Bloomington, IN 47403
www.iuniverse.com
1-800-Authors (1-800-288-4677)

ISBN: 978-1-4401-1528-8 (sc)
ISBN: 978-1-4401-1529-5 (ebook)

Printed in the United States of America

iUniverse rev. date: 1/13/2009

To Mom & Dad

Thanks for making my life poetry
I simply record it

Contents

Introduction

I took an interest in foxes when I met one in a dream. While this might sound uncommon, nothing could be further from the truth. In Native American legends, foxes often appear to test and trick animals. In Japanese mythology, the *kitsune* take the shape of humans, not to trick us, but to explore their three favorite subjects: fire, love, and hope.

That fox, the one I met in an echo of yesterday, told me my first poem.

Dreams, he said, are like raindrops on the windowpane. Sometimes they come too many and shatter too quick. The bigger ones linger and slide like tears down the glass. No matter how we reach for them, we'll never get near enough. If we close our eyes, we can hear them, we can smell them, our lips become cold on the pane, but we'll never hold them.

That sounded like a nightmare, until things started to fade. I woke up with tears on my face. Can you cry while sleeping? Then I remembered the last words of that fox …

"Don't be afraid," he said. "Open the window."

There were raindrops on my face.

What you hold here is a collection of poems inspired by the spirit and myths of foxes and their favorite themes. Will these poems trick you? Will they test you? Will they make you think of mist-filled forests or twilight fields? Only the pages will tell. Just know, my intentions couldn't be further from the truth.

Several of the poems contained within are from longer works, novels and screenplays. A brief synopsis of each can be found at the end of this book.

Thank you for reading. Thank you for dreaming.

— *Brian David Granatir*

1. A Thousand Steps Away

When I met the soldier with eyes of blue
He stepped forward and said a strange thing
"Fifty thousand, eight hundred and thirty two"
And smiled as he kissed my ring

With a salute, and a hand put to his sword
He turned and promptly walked away
And with each of his steps taken afterward
He continued to count and pray

At first, I thought my ears were mistaken
When I heard the soldier with eyes of blue
Had counted every single step he'd taken
In his journey away from you

Then I took interest, as no commander should
And began to ask about one of my men;
The blacksmith recalled as best he could,
"Forty-nine thousand and ten.

"His tears fell and hissed upon my anvil
When he handed me his broken sword
As he came a hundred paces from battle
Where his first kill had been scored."

Next, I overheard some ladies' gossip
About this soldier with eyes of blue
The nurse said she almost made his love slip
And made him forget about you

"We spoke of love beneath a sky of red
And to tease him, I stepped towards the sun
He hesitated, followed, and softly said,
Ninety-five thousand and one."

Lastly, it was the priest who spoke to me
And said this was a strange fellow indeed,
"I found him dying beneath an oak tree
Where red leaves fall and bleed

"He said Death his promise must enshrine
And so he stumbled and staggered to stand
Ninety-nine thousand, nine hundred, ninety-nine
Oh dear God: One hundred thousand."

It was then that my war and life grew dim
And I lost thought of your lover true
Until when, in my last battle, I saw him
The soldier with eyes of blue

Like all the pieces, he lay fallen too
So I ran, ran through the chaos mounting
Grabbed his chest and shouted, "At least you,
YOU CANNOT STOP COUNTING!"

As he stood, he gave a smile so serene
And said, "Two hundred thousand and thirteen."
I said, "Two hundred thousand and fourteen."
"No," he replied, "and twelve, my king."

With his steps faltering and his life undone
I threw down my sword, ripped off my crown,
Went under his arm, and walked as one

"Count down," I said, "your trip is done."

The steps were mine and the count was his
On and on we went to where his heart lives
And when he slept—as he strength gives—
My mouth and count became his

He whispered in my ear all the strange things
That happened along his many steppings
I fight and fought back the tears it brings
Oh this life not meant for kings

We stopped amidst a field so very dear
An important promise was given here—
We collapsed beneath a lonely birch tree—
He promised to come back to thee

He said a soldier's duty was to die
But for him this fate would not apply
For as sure as the sky or his eyes were blue
He promised to marry you

But cruel, cruel world, he did not fail
I came to you to give this one detail
For it was my strength, not his, that stopped
When in that golden field we dropped

I know you'd rather have a soldier than a king
Especially one who has done such a thing
One who kept the soldier with eyes of blue
Kept him but a thousand steps away from you

Oh what agony is it to know of this great hero
Who never got a chance to say, "Zero."

2. By the Petal Falling

In a carafe upon on my desk
Stood a solitary rose
Its shape statuesque
Its color bold

Alone, it grew to fill that space
Crowding my desk and its world
Around that small vase
It unfurled

Sadly, nothing lasts forever
And by the petal falling
This sweet endeavor
Found its ending

But still it was (with strength undone
And a back all broke and bent;
Spilt of its crimson)
Magnificent

Oh rose, it was not by your surrender
That your days were pushed aside
Oh rose, your splendor
It never dies

Because here, it forever lies

3. *Ten*

The chest and arm of a birch tree shone bright
In the crimson light of the fallen sun
Save for the dark spot where our backs held tight
On opposite sides of a young trunk

On the eastward wind, her words were carried
Quickly past my ears, whispers overwhelmed
The "shush" echoed as the wind was married
To the nearby creek which babbled and swelled

Her voice had so few opportunities
But does it matter what we had to say?
There will always be tomorrow for me …
But sadly, tomorrow never is today

> Was it just infatuation?
> Was there anything between you and me?
> Through the curse of separation
> The price of love is an eternity

Before disappearing in my shadow
The bleeding leaves glittered above my head
Memories, catch the twilight as you go
The birch trees are forever red

> They say the memories will someday fade
> That lie is something a hero can fight
> I will not forget, I am not afraid
> I'll gladly live forever in our night

Oh how many possibilities lied
Separated by the width of a birch tree
Oh how many uncertainties died
with her … just ten inches from me

~

The Virginia Round-Leaf Birch was the first tree put on the Endangered Species list.

The entire population lives along a small creek in southwest Virginia.

Scientists debate whether this is the end of a species or just the beginning of a new one.

4/16/07

4.

As my candle grows shy
I am angered by what never came
Oh this simple little sigh
The hiss of water on the flame

5.

The water spilt on this section
Carries a mirror in its tracks
Oh is that my reflection
Slipping through the cracks

6.

The spark of every man's life
Comes from the impact of two swords
Their clash is our very strife
And their separation our reward

7. A Traveler's Heart

There will be that one step. It might come to you in the middle of the road, or in the shadow of a hemlock tree, but it will come. You'll stop for what seems like no reason at all, look back, and remember things barely noticed. The girl who passed you on the bridge. A village left in the mountains. The insignificant, the memories of a glance, will fill you with questions of what might have been. True love? A home? Purpose. It will be then, at that point, when you must decide. Will you take that next step? If you do, if you take that chance, then you will be a true traveler, my friend. Nothing else will stop you, and you'll take with you a battle—a battle that will rage in your heart—a brilliant, ceaseless battle of possibilities and regret.

8. *Everything Fades*

Your steps fall in the snow
Where my footprints once were.
Because it is easier to follow
You go where the path is tread.
Yet, like a howl in the night,
And wheat beneath the blades,
On this path that I lead,
Everything fades.

9. Love and Hate

The brightest moon
The darkest night
Like a wolf all black
And a tiger white

What could frame thy fearful symmetry
And put your scope in the same great sigh

(a) A Forest of Silver

Wandering through shafts of light and dark,
I found myself lost, in a forest of bamboo
Like paper white beneath the poet's mark,
Through black lines, I glimpse a moonlit hue

The slowly drifting leaves, tapered as they are,
Glint silver and disappear like shooting stars

When the wind stops, I stop beside her
And in silence, my eyes see something stir
The lines move, the pages tear, with a tiger
Her grace and glory wrapped in palest fur

White tiger, white tiger, are you splendor
Or a gentle huntress, waiting for surrender

Oh to stroke that fur and touch her softly
To feel the untamed heartbeat beating
To sneak up from behind and take her quickly
And feel those strong muscles teasing

White tiger, white tiger, are you splendor
Or a lonely soul, waiting for surrender

Tell me, tell me, stop your hunt and tell me
Shout into this forest silver, shout at this page
Cry through these bars and answer my plea
Please tell me and free me from thy cage

White tiger, white tiger, are you splendor
Or an endless dream, waiting for surrender

Curse your silence and curse your reading
Answer me, you horrid beast, before you go
Why deny my touch, deny this pleading
Don't go, stay with me, my love … don't go

White tiger, white tiger, are you splendor
Or a distant love, waiting, waiting, waiting

Waiting for my surrender

(b) A Forest of Gold

In the midst of a lucent autumn day
Beneath a blue sky framed with gray,
I entered a forest where children play,
A place forgotten,
To hunt a hunting wolf gone astray.

I did not notice all the leaves then
Falling from their branches rotten—
Birch, oak, plum, ash, and aspen
The color of gold—
Drifting like angel feathers fallen.

Only during a gust of biting cold
Was the truth of these leaves told
As their wet forms took their hold
On slick black bark
And my dark skin so equally bold.

I tried to free myself from their mark,
But two took hold for each I tore apart.
A drowning my golden sea did impart
When he did appear
With piercing eyes and fur so dark.

The sight locked me with great fear.
He moved free like a ship in the clear
While I was held like a statue here.
How could it be done?
The leaves slid from his black veneer.

Oh those eyes, those eyes of a demon
Like a sunset in that dying season.
Oh that smile shining without reason.
Oh my great enemy,
How can my heart take such treason?

How, oh how could I ever forget thee,
You wretch, you beast that torments me—
O wolf I hunted in a place of mystery
Who took my heart
When you showed me a way to be free?

My fate, my being, my hate, all things god foretold
Shall be trapped forever, in a forest made of gold.

10. A Poem by the Rayn

Was it by chance, or fate, or some other thing
That along this path walking; I found a rose
Cut and alone in a land were only the lilac grows?

Was it fancy, hate, or tepid woes that bore me down
To take that stately rose from off that ground
And beneath the cottonwood crowns; ask it this:

"Was it she for whom you fell, for whom you flourish?
Was it she who put you to this, left you to your misery?"
To which the red rose did blush and say to me,

"Once I knew a lady, who held me at her cheek
Near lips so soft they made my petals pale and bleak,
Who through a sigh did often speak: I love you.

"Oh to feel that touch, her touch, renew—
To be again, like so few—her object of affection,
But I cannot, and cannot I cry for her rejection

For a flower is perfection: if it were to weep."
! Was it this thorn that made me drop you to my feet
In that land of golden wheat, and struggle as I speak?

"If what you say is true, as true as I do think,
And a rose cannot drink his own sweet tears,
Then a man cannot make the love he so endears.

"Oh these long years, I have only wanted from thee

When I should have given, made you bloom, set you free;
For it does not matter if you love me: I love you.

"No, my dear flower, resting cut upon the floor,
Remember this, this alone, and nothing more:
Even if life is vain, I'll always have my love for her—
And you, you'll always have the rain."

11. The Falcons Are Falling

Here I sit in a far and distant land
My feet dangling in a ravine.
Through the tall, bearded clouds
The falcons are falling.

As one breaks from the heavens,
A wisp of fog follows his descending
And against the dark rock face
Like a shooting star, his trail is fading.

Faster and faster he falls
Towards a shining river that lies below.
At the last moment he stops
As his reflection begins to show.

His claws snap forward
His wings spread out; he decides to fly.
The reflections meet in a splash.
He denies gravity; he does not die.

In his wake, fall many more
Each followed by a cloudy chain.
And in that last moment they stop,
Turn, and fly from the mirror pane.

I stand and take a few steps back
This isn't suicide; I'm not dying—
I run I run I run and leap—
This is a man briefly flying.

My fingers pass through their chains.
As I fall, they continue to race past me.
I do not see my reflection.
The rising sun fills the river to the sea.

In the water I still live.
The bubbles rise like leaves on the wind.
One more falcon comes to the surface.
She goes deeper than her kin.

Her claws dip into the water, she reaches for me then.

I reach for her, I watch her fly; carry me to heaven.

12. Carved

My sword mimics the distant sky
Along its edge glints the setting sun
Oh, but how this horizon lies
Near me, to me—my journey's done

In the grass, near a seaward cliff
I sit against an ageless tree
Distant waves whisper, "What if …"
What if I made it home to thee

I was a villain when I left you
And for you that will never change
Some heroes never make it home
But they're heroes all the same

—carved on a birch tree

13. I Saw a Shadow

I saw a shadow chasing a petal down a stream
With a beak, feathers, and regal mien.
What a strange scene, to see a black bird there
But was it for a crow an equally peculiar thing?

To see a flower's petal floating down a stream
Along this curb in the city of forgotten dreams.

Then, like a forcefully interrupted prayer,
My telltale guide was forced to stop there
At a dam unfair, where the water was contained
In a pool, at the ankle of a young girl's sneaker.

With her hands and face lost in a curtain of wet hair,
It's no wonder she didn't see a crow's despair.

Her eyes then went up to a sun unrestrained,
Tearing through clouds that recently reigned,
But all was in vain, for a sun cannot break through
The building's unforgiving, concrete frame.

And what of that last drop of fallen rain
That traces her cheek like a tear unchained?

Why, why I had no idea of what to do.
My guide moved and grasped the petal at the shoe
And off he flew, towards the sun beyond the city
Towards a golden field and sky of fading blue.

And on I went, on down that simple avenue
In the city where a shadow caught my view.

Oh, will someone ever take you
Off to that place so very true
Where the crow and his dear petal flew

14. Referendum

I did not know which way I had fallen
Until I hit the bottom
And glimpsed ever briefly the sky

Yours,
—Aza

15. Through the Door

She pauses at the end of the hall; she lingers in the
light. The gap between them closes slowly—that glow is
dimming—the sharp line of the doorway and the curve
of her silhouette—two shadows merging. "Hurry,"
she says once more. Her eyes are seeking, as they are
peeking, passing through the door.

16. The Grave of Oscar Wilde

I found a poet's secret grave
Three steps across the sand
On a trip to a distant sea
Where the sweet lilies stand
Beneath that little tent of blue
Made by blue petals grand

And inscribed on a rock nearby
Two names were easily read
Above and below a cross
By a heart surrounded—
What a strange eulogy was this
What a death confounded

My mind then tried to comprehend
Oh this great lost poem
That every man writes with his end:
"Dear sir or dear madam
My life was over when it began
Cogito ergo sum

"For each is like a grain of sand
With a life so banal
That seems ruled by the tide
With no control at all
For whom originality
Seems but impossible

"Oh my little speck of sand
A moment will come by
When carried by wind and chance
Into a lover's eye
You'll live in such happiness
And make her think to cry

"Then you'll fall, as all things should
Past her cheek to the air
Back to your heedless brothers
And darken the ground there
Until you dry in the sun
And finally disappear."

Still of this, life's great sad poem,
There was one who smiled
Tipped his hat and declared
Life is not so mild
And lived a different poem
Who lived truly wilde

Grains of sand are not defined
By that far seaward land
Instead, my friend, it is that shore
Made magnificent by the sand
For every man lives to realize
His own potential grand

Oh live, live like a grain of sand
To ride upon the wind
To lie beneath the lilies' bow
To sit upon a poet's brow

Oh live, live to life's sweet demand
To love and love again
To journey in the sea and sun
And until your very end
… be wilde

17. Autumn Leaves Can Cry

Although the leaves shine bright
On the dark branches high
Death mars such a beautiful sight
Because autumn leaves can cry

In summer and in spring
Their lips drink the raindrops
But now they linger and they cling
To the back of colored spots

Oh yellow, brown, and red
So many eyes are swollen
Their tears trace a path to the dead
Where too they will be fallen

I fear failure (now and then)
And so often it finds me
Even as I write this poem
Beneath an autumn tree crying

A leaf is prettier than a petal
When at last it says goodbye
But no one can ever tell
Because autumn leaves can cry

18. The Moonflower Vine

Tripping, rising, running, falling through a castle in the night,
I follow the fire fleeting, as the wind attacks the torchlight.
Like a sailor, I search for a shore at every distant glimmer,
But I can never stop, with the world as my conspirator.

Like a piano player gone deaf or a painter gone blind,
My tormentor is of the particular and brutal kind.
Fingertip memories and lost possibilities prevail
In this misery and memory of my dear sweet Abigail.

I think I see someone at the end of the hall, a guard perhaps,
But his eyes are muted by the lightning flash! So Heaven cracks.
My footsteps are lost as well, in the span of echoing thunder;
No one will ever catch me, with the world as my conspirator.

No words, no colors, no comparison can explain her beauty,
This angel who was first to see nothing common in me.
But alas, our love and those autumn days were to no avail,
For the Prince was avowed to marry a princess named Abigail.

The scent, her scent of lilies grown in the hot time of
spring,
Draws me suddenly from the hall to a dark place
flowering.
Such a detour saves me from the knightly mob rushing
to her.
My escape was not by chance; the world is my
conspirator.

As the arrow of a hungry hunter flies towards anything
And a well-fed man follows the orders of a madcap
king,
I thought my desperate heart alone drew me along your
fair trail,
But I was wrong: our love was true love, my dear sweet
Abigail.

Crushing such delicate things, I fall through a midnight
garden.
Have you finally given up on me? My world, is this our
end?
But then my hands catch the taille, hem, and busk of a
hanging vine,
And I find white flowers blooming through these dark
fingers of mine.

Your half-set smile and glancing eyes played message
boy to our love.
Like the moonflower our passion grew without blessings
from above.
But I kept my promise to you, I kept our promise
without fail

To hold you in my arms for the rest of your life, sweet
Abigail.

Dear world, my villain, you did not abandon me as I
fell,
For the blood on my hands wipes off on these soft
petals pale.
They will keep it hidden when in the morning they
close up tight.
My secret will come forth only in the deep of the night.

Madness, I can't stand this; a murderer has but one
profession.
Come take me! Guards! Guards! I don't care who falls
with my confession,
But the wind (the world) steals her name from my lips
with her able gale
As I scream and shout and yell (I loved you) my dear
sweet "Abigail!"

Tripping, rising, running, falling through a castle in the
night,
Like an arrow, nothing can save me from my dreadful
flight.
With the world as my jailer, and all our lost love as
blackmail,
Every day will be hell without you … my dear, dear
sweet Abigail

19. The Echo of Raindrops

A man stands in the rain
Near an acacia tree
With eyes cast towards heaven
His tears drown in the sea

Then with no warning at all
The rain's long solo ends
But this song is not quiet
Such meek silence portends

From the flowers in my hand
And from leaves overhead
By such tiny waterfalls
This cadence never ends

And in the nept of silence
And through the lack of sound
He hears her step behind him
Her hand reaching around

She steals that final note
She wipes it off his chin
Oh how long has she been there
Standing right behind him

What will come in that moment
Will their love ever stop
"Don't go," she says to him—
The echo of raindrops

20. Phoenix Fly

On a cliff, I watched a woman die
Beneath a broken storm and sunset sky
High above the slowly calming sea
She spreads her arms wide and started to sing

The world answered but not in echo
Red and gold, the clouds began to glow
Shifting and swirling, I watched them dance
Arching wings marking the phoenix's entrance

As she turned, so did the fire follow
On breaking waves, so did the shimmer grow
White splashes chased the phoenix frame
Rising steam for water in the flame

And in the sky, the highest drops lingered
Through broken clouds they slowly filtered
Fire caught in a darkening sky
Stars mark where she made the phoenix fly

That was when I started to run
Run up that hill
On slick grass my feet slipped
For her I reached
Short, by only a fingertip

On a cliff, I watched a woman die
Into the sea, I watched a phoenix fly
If it wasn't real, why did I feel a warmth breath
And hum that song until my own death

21. A Subtle Passing

In her garden, we planted an iris
and like our love, we slowly watched it grow
Every inch marked a moment of our bliss
Until our feet encouraged us to go

On a journey over the sea so blue
Thermonasty—heat made the flowers bloom
But before our return, they wilted too
Their pointed stalks marking a lover's tomb

I knew the iris blooms at night back then
But never thinking I'd miss all of her
Although I have long since left that garden
I can't help but remember our flower

Like young love blooming, what has gone unseen?
Was my life a boon or subtle passing?

22. Night Fall

One night, I saw all the stars fall
Streaking, lingering through my tears
Stretched by my slowly squinting eyes
So all of heaven disappears

It may sound like I'm a hero
Strong enough to conquer the sky
But that night I was a failure
Who let a promise slowly die

I promised myself I wouldn't sleep
Not until I held you again
But you're so far away, my love
Even if you're in my heart and head

One night, I saw all the stars fall
The whole world slowly went black
Consumed by a dreamer's desire
For you, my love, to come back

23. The Girl of the Doorway

How many times have I sat here waiting
Debating the promise of an empty door
How long have I been anticipating
Hoping to see her once more

Oh that lovely form whose traces stalk me
Whose voice I hear in every sound and silence
Whose hair sways needles of a sunset tree
And fills the fringe of evanescence

The frame is empty since her departure
A blank canvas where only memories stray
How long have I sat here waiting for her:
The girl of the doorway

Like a tiger, she carries the dawn into the night
Through eyes that are both bold and bright
And through darker streaks meant for play
Like a tiger, she carries the dusk into the day

With lips meant to whisper and angel wings
A silhouette grows from the edge of the doorframe
Her movements and her words are subtle things
Like the shadows of a flame

My love, she fills the promise of an empty door
And even if she leaves as before
There is no greater task or fate
Then to sit and stay, to wait and anticipate

The girl of the doorway

24. (1184) - The Lost Poem of Emily Dickinson

Dear Haulm,

At first, I thought it was a mistake. The small scrap of paper came alone—no letter, no note. My only clues to its origin were the initials written at the bottom and the dried flower that came with it—the petal of a foxglove.

Who? Who would send such a thing to me? I thought long and hard, and then suddenly, like the sound of the bell from the town priory, it came to me. I remembered her! It was nearly forty years ago, but certainly, if there was any day that my mind would seize, it must be this.

I remembered that moment amidst the twilight. There was an unusual fog for that time of year, between summer and fall. It lingered, and as the day came to an end, the color of the setting sun bled out through the mist, casting the world in a rosé haze. It was then, as I neared the steep slant of a verdant hill, that I saw her. The child descended on me so fast, I was afraid we might collide.

I stopped her with both hands, and we laughed. "Sorry, mister." She was an unusual child, thin and pale, with eyes like the fog. One side of her chestnut-colored hair was bound nicely by a yellow ribbon, while the other side was free to follow the indescribable rhyme of the wind. And as those strands of long hair tapped against the side of her face, I wondered where the other ribbon had gone.

With her apology lent, and my attention turned down, I thought the child would be on her way. I was surprised when she asked, "What are those for?" I finished collecting the flowers I'd recently dropped and looked up at her. "I'm taking these to the hill where the hawthorn trees grow." Then, as her hands pulled sharply at the knees of her dress, she asked, "Can I have one?"

I stood and looked at my destination. She came down that hill; how could she not know what was in my procession? "You don't want one of these flowers, my dear."

She quickly asked, "Why? What should make a flower any other thing than a flower?" She leapt forward and began to riffle through my stems, like an accountant with his pages.

Why would she want one of these? She could pick them anywhere—in the gutter by the road or near the farmer's fence. In fact, these flowers were so common that the florists refused to sell them, even in this weary time of year. Certainly, a person with money would buy something else—something better, something worthy.

"What if you outlive me?" asked the child. "Will you give me a flower then?"

I sighed and shook my head. "I won't outlive you, dear." I moved her hand and gave her a different flower instead. The purple trumpets that covered the stem matched perfectly with her fox-colored hair. She laughed and rushed away from me. Off they went, towards a world fading from red. A girl without care—away from where so many other flowers had gone. Off to a place, where I wished we would one day go. To a life of loving bliss—a life lived simplest.

Oh how often I have remembered that day, but never did I remember that girl until this. When this scrap of paper arrived, I thought at first it was from a misfit. Then I thought it was perhaps from an angel. Then, when I finally recognized what it was, I thought it was a gift.

It is often the nature of men to be greedy, and maybe that's why I kept this hidden for so long. I've never been a rich man, but at least I had this one rare thing—not the poem, but her sweet, sweet memory.

Yours,

—M. Barlowe

P.S. I'm sorry for the smudges. When first I read this, I was standing in the shadow of a early spring rain.

~

How is love to be ascribed—
	To the Flea, the Raven, or the snake—
Many things have carried it,
	But for me and my mistakes
It shall be a Vulture
	For whom love partakes

Oh think it strange
	To see them flock to death,
When we do it all the same
	While angels rest;
Give ferocious shrieks and cries
	With every breath

When is a flower deemed ugly
	When is a bird deemed mad
When is an hour lost
	And a child sad
Oh Eternity marred with death
	Made love a lover's fad

It is on the wings of a vulture
	That I am taken to You—
Carried from the hawthorn trees
	High up to heaven—
Oh what sweet mysteries
	Await us—upon that breeze

25. *The Smell of Ice*

On a park bench meant for waiting
In the twilight of a late morning
I watched the children play

They ran between the grassy bends
Kicking frost from leaf and stems
Green beneath the gray

The fingers that lay upon my face
With breathe escaping their embrace
Hid a smile away

Oh that laughter how it flowed
With a chorus that echoed
Children from yesterday

Then as I rose to my feet
I turned and looked at my seat
A shadow did stay

For upon that bench covered in ice
Was a small shape held so precise
Where my body lay

By the tips of my back and arms
Was this smaller shape made like a child
Waiting to play

And I watched in the warmth of day
As that shape grew and faded away
With a smile I accepted the advice
Breathed deep the smell of ice

26. Share This Moment

I think of her and I wonder
Will she share this moment with me?
There is so much that I'd show her
But will she think it fantasy?

I know that only time will tell
If these thoughts will ever echo
Like the sweet melody that I whistle
To the songbird out my window

27.

A bird landed on my side
As I slept beneath the willow
In a whisper it lied
Making me think yesterday …
                was tomorrow

28.

Oh my lonely heart is enticed
By moonlight misunderstood
Such passion goes unnoticed
Like foxes mating in the wood

29. The Emerald Valley

If a man must die, let him do so here
In the valley where seasons change the year.
Oh, let him stand between the mountains tall
And at his horse's ending find landfall,

Where the sea and the rivers come to play
In a kingdom called Kalay.

Beneath the boughs of endless birch and oak,
Between the swaying light and shadow's cloak,
Where every bird, upon these branches high,
Knows your name and sings a whispered sigh,

May he see the fields of wheat assembled
In this valley of the Emerald.

Children and lilies play in daylight hours,
Near the shadows of a castle's towers.
In their laughter and in their play, one hears
Echoes of that famous Prince's tears.

If a man must die, let him do so here
In the valley where seasons change the year.

Here, only one child cries each day,
In a kingdom called Kalay.

—A Children's Poem

30. Ode to a Shattered Statue

I.

What horror, what tragedy is this,
That the rising sun should unveil
That yesterday was madness
And an artist's convictions fail

In his studio lie the piteous pieces
Of palest marble with greenest vein,
Each of the fragment leases
The form of a lovely lady's frame

Her long hair lies tossed in the corner,
As if cut by mourning shears
And at the large and capacious door
Lie her curious, tilted ears

At her toes is the shroud of Leander
That draped her chest so bare
Under the bench, her fingers slender
Twist anxious at a spider's hair

In the shadow, hidden are her lips
And on them is hidden a smile
In the light are two smaller chips,
Eyes that hold a hidden guile

How many days did she spend there
And how many more will you spend;
Staring out just over his shoulder
At blue Athens skies that never end

II.

We find him collapsed beside the bed
Our murderer with hammer at his side
With a heavy, downward head
And tears waiting to be tried

Her blood is on his trembling hands
Her last breath and final sigh
On his cheeks and shoulders stands
All of it a palest powder dry

Then it starts with a twinkle in his eye
They say inspiration is a fickle thing
Making a slit through a cloudy sky
To his chin, a tear does cling

Oh watch it, watch it, watch it fall
Made of marble and artist sweat
This little statue so very, very small
In an immortal silhouette

So perfect was it for that moment
When it was meant for all to adore
This miracle that God had sent
That soon crashed upon the floor

There it lies, in fragments white
Like the eyes that lie broken
That stare forever at a far and distant light
For a statue cannot move a single limb

Even if it was just about, just about,
Just about to look at him

31. The Cinder Field

I smell the scent of distant smoke
On the crest of an autumn breeze
That perfume lingers in me
Stirring long forgotten memories

The chill in my heart melts so suddenly
With echoes of what she said, "Dance with me"

Lovers meet in the cinder field
Among the tall cotton flowers
And with a passion growing
Turning and turning, they dance for hours

Black—thru the night of each other's shadow
Light—they pass to and from the sunset glow

Their step and sway stirs the embers
Around them fireflies are flowing
And while nigh is almost night
Their fire is forever growing

Black to light, by such love the phoenix flies
Soon the world is consumed and embers rise

The flecks of light stall in the sky
The darkest ash is all we see
Except for the stars above
Caught on the tux of eternity

In the dark she whispers softly to him
"I love you," this is how the world ends

Lovers meet in the cinder field
To dance and burn the world away
And even if life is fleeting
That light, their passion, will never fade

I smelled the scent of distant smoke today
And our love didn't seem so far away
Locked and trapped in a place of memory
Where I loved you and you loved me

32. Melt the Frost

The latest frost of my youthful life
Came well in the middle of spring,
And for the blooms that could not close tight
Stems and leaves soon filled with winter rife
And their pale ghosts waited for morning;
Although the ice made each flower a gem
That shone with a strong majestic light,
I could not help but find horror then
To see the wrong season in my garden,
And know not everything will be right
If I touch their petals or their leaves
My warmth and oily mark will linger
The ice will melt and again they'll breathe,
But my embrace is a curse it seems
The ones I touch won't bloom again this year;
I don't care, I'll kiss each one slowly
So die by fire instead of ice;
The latest frost of my life touched me
And ever since I've not bloomed fully
Even if my springtime came twice

33. The Poet and the Princess

Upon the board beneath your feet
A tear did settle
Does the flower smell as sweet
Having lost a petal

~

A poet speaks of flowers
As a minute speaks of hours
In winter, what must he say then
Amid the chills and showers

I remember them

~

For a poet this taste is very bitter
He does not make the flowers beautiful
It is your memories that give them grandeur
A sin
He hopes that you're some great fool
To mistake a sparrow for a violin

~

Maybe this little caged bird
Wants her foolish heart spurred
So thin, looking through bars so narrow
She calls for a poetic word

Oh violin …
Can you be my sparrow?

~

I'll break this cage with my sword
I'll throw you towards the sky
But I don't know a single word
That can show you how to fly

I'll put you on my shoulder
I'll climb the mountain high
We will leap from that boulder
And together we will die

But for a brief moment, you will fly

~

What if in your great leap
I found strength so very deep

What if from your grasp I flew
Would you cry, would you weep

Would you know what to do
Would you still say, I love you?

~

Fly

34. For Lady Emilia Lanier

When the sun sets amid the bells of morn
And at their closing drapes a dusky stage,
Oh thy black silk hair flies to watchers warn
And writes sweet lines upon the cloudy page.

Such a sad story many players bring.
True Beauty fair shall be thy very queen
And Sorrow thy knave and Fortune thy king.
Thy lovers are Mirth, although rarely seen.

But thy rogue, by lies, oft is Flattery.
Finally, Love is thy great patron's lendings.
Men dream and long for such a fantasy
Although tales are defined by their own endings

Yet to have never writ this story of thee
Shall remain my life's singular tragedy.

35. Every Path in Winter

Every path in winter is the same.
The deepest rut and form of every tree
Beneath a sheet of pure white snow
Hold the same shape equally.

Sand and stone and the ice of a lake
All feel the same beneath my walking feet
And every horizon is bright
Beneath a sky that is always bleak.

With eyes cast towards heaven, I feel it melt
I feel it converting into rain
On my cheeks, the warmth of my skin
Changes snowflakes into tears again

The footsteps I find match the ones I left
And every twist and turn is indifferent.
But beneath this winter season
The changes are magnificent.

And what of this savior, on whose stump I rest
Taken to die in a place without trees
But through shimmering ornaments
A pine tree finally gets her leaves

The setting sun in this season echoes
Candlelight shining bright at midday
Oh how we hope the light whispers
Bring us the New Year for which we pray

Even this moment is going to change
I can't wait for our words to shift from "Someday"
When your doubts are overwhelmed
To when I can finally say

"I'm home"

Every path in winter is the same
I'm not lost
The deepest ruts, the shape of every tree
I'm just far away
Every footstep, every twist and every bend
Leads to our someday

Every path in winter is the same
And there's only one thing for me to do
On and on I keep going
Because every path leads me home to you

36. Platinum Lake

Like a whisper in the dark
What a strange sound comes to me
While out for an evening swim
I hear a cello play incessantly

The concerto grows louder
Coming from a distant shore
What harmony in silence
As the orchestra waits to play once more

Even the wind takes a seat
In the crowded row of trees
And the scent of icy smoke
Slips from the wet lips biting at my knees

Everything is muted gray
Save for where one color lies,
Molten lead, above the haze,
The sunset fills cracks in the cloudily skies

Things grow cold, that color fades
I try but I can't reach heaven
For upon a seamless mirror
I am nothing more than a reflection

Stars hang from an angel's tongue
Such are the day's last moments
But there are these cords of hope
That echo of a tenor's performance

But then, oh then, the cello stops
And I become trapped; I become numb
For there can be no ripple
For a man in a lake made of platinum

37. A Moment Past the Garden

As I depart the company of flowers
I am stopped by a sorrowed call.
It is the turtledove's voice that sours
That precious moment so very small

When done with my day's work
I exit through the garden wall

And yet, his cry makes me weaken
Pause for a while there at the edge
In the scent of rosemary and cyclamen
Lily, rose, mint, and magnolia hedge

A symphony of flower scents
To overwhelm a bird's song and pledge

It is in those dyeing scents that I recall
The past, of things growing and grown
Of life in winter, summer, spring, and fall
But it is not memories that I take home

It is the countless possibilities
Of what might yet grow

Still, there is this song of the turtledove
Who, as legend says, will not sit on green
Or sing again to replace his lost love
Why, in my garden, can't he be seen?

What might he see in me
To make him want to love again?
I linger only a second in life's nobility
In the sweet breath of blooms unburdened
Filled with joy and joyful possibility
With only one bird's mourning to pardon

The whole world lies before me
In that moment past the garden

38. A Momentary Wish

A song of beauty hangs on your lips
And in each silence I wait for this
For you to end that fragile thing
And complete my momentary wish

Sing

39. Tuesday

Oops, Tuesday has come so fast
It was taken
By the cat sleeping in my lap
And the rain sliding down the glass
By the bird sitting on the fence post
Whose feathers mark the wind's pass
I pause my writing to send a message
To a friend I simply must harass

For as the bird's wing is for the breeze
My mind was meant for you
And days like these

40. A Dying Prince's Lullaby

The moon soars high above me, right above me
As I sit alone beneath the lilac tree.
The sweat of grass and chill breath of wind,
Like all my other lovers, abandon me here.

The world is still and silent for this drifting soul.
Although it's night, there is no tomorrow.
And all the stars' whispers have gone astray,
Since I cannot push the loud moon away.

But what, what is that, if not a star I see
Dangling on a strand of silk above me?
No, close to my eye is this little blur,
But still I recognize the form of a spider.

Why do you linger above me, why do you sway?
What makes you float on this windless day?
Did you come for my warmth, like all the rest,
Or did you come simply to ride my breath?

Go, my little prince, mount my thermals and fly,
Be a moonlit kite in the darkened sky.
Was I ever like this, living on someone's sighs,
Whispers, gasps, moans, shouts, and lies?

Although you're far from your kingdom, I won't forget.
Go on, my little prince, and live without regret.
Have no destination, my little spider
Then you can survive, somehow survive, without her.

Then comes a shadow and blocks out the moon.
Why have you come to take me so soon?
I can see the stars now, but the spider's gone,
And I wonder … whose breath did I live upon?

41. To the Sky

My niece dances with a leaf
Picks it up and flings it high
Such a journey is so brief
From the ground back to the sky

Sadly, everything must fall
Still, she twirls with him
And waving her hands so small
For a leaf, she makes the wind

Oh, if our life be like this
When we fall, we fall together
Knowing that moment of bliss
When we elevate each other

Being lifted up so very high
Over and over ... back to the sky

42. The Second Light

Here I sit, at a window, in the middle of the night
With two shapely glows of flickering candlelight
That flip back and forth like a cat's touched ear
Yet only one flame is real, with a wick to shear
The other a reflection, on the glass a glow so slight.

Then, at this dark hour, thoughts of my love appear
And memories of us standing on a shore draw near.
At the sea, where silky waves waltzed upon our feet,
I saw the sun, like this fire, in a perfect mirror repeat,
The bluer sea and darker night of your eyes so clear.

Next, I asked in jealousy, "If all your eyes will treat
Is this sun fair, then blind you'll go, taken by deceit
And think this night, this dusk, forever does exist.
Would you prefer your eye my image forever miss?
Do you want this, my dear, for your love to compete?"

My breath caught as I waited for her to answer this.
Oh what horror, my heart, to see that smile amiss,
To think that she might prefer the sun over the sea,
To have tears for wrong reasons when she said to me,
"I don't need eyes, my sweet, even the blind can kiss."

Like this candle, my love glows brightest for thee
Oh my beautiful angel which the heavens set free …

Then—at a gust of horrid wind—my candle dims.
Only my grasp keeps the room from darkness grim.
What a fragile light as this! Brings a thought to me

For as one light did fade, so did another grow slim.
One light, one reflection, relies on the other's whim.
Could it be the same for love? I wonder with a shiver,
Could her love be but a reflection of love given to her?
Can it be, that he loves her, but she loves not him?

Is my love so bright? Am I such a willing giver?
Can I not see the shadow because of light I render?
Oh God, what if I blow out this one candle here—
Is the other doomed and destined to disappear?
Does she love him? I must know. Oh my lips do quiver.

As to a candle, I blow a kiss and douse a tear ...
Black. So dark. Like the night that children fear.
I sit here for a moment, in this land without sight,
My eyes, my heart, my soul still remembering the light.
Oh will I ever see you, hold you, know you again, my dear?

Without my love for you
Unless ... a second light appear

43. The Flower of Heaven

It started on a Tuesday.

I was standing outside my home, looking at a twilight
horizon. I missed the sun, but it still lit the sky with
memories of the day. The light shone through a small
slit, caught between the dark clouds that hung like
mountains on the horizon and the wisps that hung like
ribbons in the air.

It was there, in the layers of light, that I saw the flower.

The stem grew through the line of green that clung to
the mountains. Its petals branched out through the
brilliant blush of red. And this flower, this rose made of
twilight, reached. It reached for the highest part of the
sky and the golden light of a dreamer's sun.

The birds must have noticed this flower too. I heard
them as they flew past, their calls and songs marching
in a parade toward a glorious sky. Oh what a wonder:
to hear these small animals deny the winter, to see their
forms break across the flower of heaven, with no worry
or care given to the coming night.

Then, of all the things this sight could stir, I thought
of you. My mind went adrift and I thought of you.
I thought of my friend, who lives in a far-off land.
I thought of people I've never met, who help make
me who I am. I thought of possibilities, promises—
probabilities and chance. Oh all these people I've

known and never met. Oh all these friends I've taken and never held. Oh all these things that are real to me.

People say that faith is dead. They say that technology has given truth and freed us from promises. It's a lie. I've never met you. I've never held you in my arms, I've never seen your smile, I've never wiped a tear from your cheek, but I know you. And I keep you, deep in my heart.

For all I know, you could be an angel, and perhaps you are. You could be a dragon or a fox that has learned to type. You could be a convict or a figment of my mind. You could be anything, but you will always be my friend. Why? Because I don't need to see you to be with you.

I found it in you. I find a soul there, I find a heart ... I find a flower.

I have faith, and faith will always have me. You have taught me love and friendship are boundless things. (Forever, thank you.) And how can I think that even the berth of eternity can change this?

And so, Tuesday finally came to an end.

I wish I could tell you that flower never wilted. I wish I could tell you that every time I look to the horizon it is covered in green, red, and gold, but I cannot. The night came, as it always does. The birdsongs grew silent, and the stars came into the world. I made a wish on one. I made a wish for you, my imaginary friend.

I can't tell you what it was, but know I'll always reach for you.
I'll reach for you as the sunset flower reached for a false sun.
I'll reach for you as the birds reached for an imaginary spring.
But I promise you, my faith, my love, will never fade.

44. A Cold Cup of Coffee
—an Angela Atten poem

Alone in a crowd at 6 AM
I hum the song you taught me
Standing in line at a walkup window
Waiting for coffee

With a chill, the sky keeps on fallin'
The shiver sets me off key
Stolen from my lips, taken by snowflakes
The song goes softly

With a curse, I take a swipe at them
Unharmed, the snow drifts from me
Behind, some girl whispers, "Didn't you know?
She's always cranky."

I turn to yell, but then I see him
The sight of a couple's glee
As they huddle in warmth to fight the snow.
Am I so lonely?

> Your memory is useless to me
> Like a cold cup of coffee
> You keep me going,
> You keep me strong,
> But there's nothing left for me
> The warmth is gone

> Our first kiss warmed my lips
> Like a cold cup of coffee

From my heart to my hips
You sent a shiver though me
But like your breath on my skin
That memory is fadin'

"She's been cynical ever since then."
It continues behind me,
"Ever since her boyfriend died long ago,
She's been so bitchy."

So forgettable, our history
Like a cold cup of coffee
Everything is more sweet
Since I met you
But it is cheap, and easy
To get something new

I don't know who or what I am
Why did this happen to me?
I just don't want to be alone, now go!
Just leave me be …

You kept me up all night
Like a cold cup of coffee
But for some reason it seemed right
To have that excitement in me
And what a joy it was too
To start each day with you

Alone in a crowd at 6 AM
I fight our memory
Standing in line at a walkup window
Waiting for coffee

45. By the Petal Fallen

I crush a small vase
To hold the stem of a rose
The shards reflecting my face
Change thorns into gentle foes

At my fingertips

Would veins show such mercy
To melt the flower petals
Would a rose be so thirsty
To drink my blood as it settles

Kiss these soulless lips

Did the world end today
If it did, I didn't notice
But I thank you anyway
For starting a new reality like this

Deny the eclipse

46. The Daisy and the Dandelion

If there is some great eternal whisper
That tickles the ears of all things to be
Before they emerge from earth or water
"Survive" is what it says to thee

All that has a beginning fears the end
And they develop a strange arsenal
To protect that life they must defend
Or risk missing that one great call

Some develop a deadly poison within
And are judged by their colors worn
Some give up the gentlest affection
And develop a sharp set of thorns

Some develop a shell over their skin
And never run beneath the skies
Some never get caught dreaming
And develop unsleeping eyes

Still, none of these quite contest
With another type of protection
For beauty and love are the best
And this is true perfection

Why?

Because Man heard that whisper too
It echoes through his every fiber
And, unsure of what he should do,
He crushes all who threaten his answer

Yet we do not pull out the weeds
That have the loveliest of flowers
We do not scold a kitten's deeds
When they make a brief love ours

And that is why I cannot love you
My dear sweet flower beneath the sun
I just don't know what to do
So I must not favor this dandelion

No, the daisy gets my sweet kiss
For it carries beauty all over its skin
Although you can take my wish
And put it on the wind

So here I take your life on bend and knee
And all I ask is that you please, please, please
Find a way to "Survive" me

47. The Standing Tree

Do you know them? Do you see them,
Those trespassers both young and old
Who stand beneath your branch and stem
And look to where the skies unfold?

Why do they come? Why come to you?
Is it that sight that lies beyond
That wild field of a wild hue
Where birds leap, like fish from a pond?

Their plumes beneath the plumes of wheat
Through the gold, the shadows swimming
When to make the moment complete
They leap towards a sun that's setting

In winter; when the days were short
It was the elderly who came
From your bark his hand stole support
His youth echoed in your frame

That girl, the one from his memories
She came during the months of spring
Her hair danced in the gentle breeze
And your whispers made her sing

That song, that sweet, sweet melody
Was remembered in summer days
Mimicked by nesting chickadees
For a young man who lost his way

Their child, the son I never had
Came in fall and stood in your lee
Bravery was learned by that lad
As he stepped out and chased your leaves

That hero …

Why you? Why not me?
What strength, what hope, do people find
From standing by this old oak tree
That stands alone where the road ends

As my ax bites into your side
I feel the flesh beneath the bark
A wicked grin slips my lips wide
As your feathers trace a graceful arc

Crack! The echo of my sins return
Racing back from distant mountains
Such things do the birds spurn
Fleeing before the silence begins

I feel it; I feel your true strength
Through the handle and through my soul
Again with my hand at arm's length—
Earth, sun, death, sky, life—I stole

I am sorry; please forgive me
But I want to see that field from my window
I am old, I am bitter, I am lonely
And I need the wood to make my fire grow

Die; the second strike is my damnation
Crack! My tears are not a confession—
Die—but the last meal of this execution
Crack! I'll write a poem on your skin

They will come, but I will not answer them
They will ask why I did such a thing to thee
Someday they will know the truth of men
That we are jealous of a tree

For a tree needs very little for his life and limb
Except, that once in a while,
        … you stand beside him

48. Eternity's Coat Man

Once I found my way to a most peculiar door
With "Forever" written in gold letters on the floor
At the end of a street I'd never walk before.

Then, ahead of my knock, someone did implore
With a clearing of his throat that I could not ignore
"I must take your hat, before you go through this door."

He snickered as I handed him my head's decor
And he gave me a claim ticket marked 1184,
A plain card like many I'd seen before.

"I must ask," he said with a deep-throated roar,
"That you do not look on the back of yours,
For an Idea is written on the back of that score,

"An Idea so great, so grand, that it could end all war,
Cure all the sickness that your people abhor,
Make you someone the universe will adore."

Then, with a creak, he took the handle on that door
And motioned for me to walk past Forever.
"All of it. All of it. All of it is for you to explore."

But this opportunity, this Idea, how could I ignore?
For the chance, the simple dream, to have the power
Of a King, and have all such glory in my store—

"I want my hat back."

"Ticket?" he said with a grin that cut to my core,
With a dispiriting laugh that made my very soul sore,
And put out an unwavering hand for card 1184,

And as I put it in his palm, I turned it over.
What I saw there filled me with such horror—
The back of that card blank, blank like Elysium's shore

Immortal sin
Ashes to ashes
Dust in the wind

Oh dear god, what dream did I put my faith in

49. The Dream Horse

The rising sun fills the world with jewels
As dewdrops on grass-backs sparkle in the light.
When the day grows warm, these gems do shatter,
Filling the field with the dust of diamonds white.

The songbirds herald the Dream Horse at dawn.
Marching from the horizon, she can't be missed.
At her head is a crown of pointed light.
On her shoulders is a cape of morning mist.

Her coat and her mane are dark and dapple
As if she runs beneath the oak-leaf shadow.
And by the freckles on her tail and cheeks
Past embers sway and sparks of the future glow.

Chasing a hawk that flies high above her,
She runs beneath an endless morning sky.
And as she watches his slow escaping,
She dreams of a day, someday, when she will fly.

Eating the grass that is still sweet with dew,
At noon, she rests beneath the cherry tree.
And as the petals stick to her soft fur,
She dreams of a day, someday, when she'll pull free.

Plunging her hooves into puddles and streams,
After noon, she keeps the world from drying.
And as water clings to her face and cheeks,
She dreams of a day, someday, worth her crying.

Racing shadows that are ever growing,
At sunset, she runs through golden grass surreal.
And as she glances at her silhouette,
She dreams of a stallion in a distant field.

You don't need him; you don't need anyone.
Oh my dear sweet Dream Horse, always be free.
Dream, hope, live, and play. Sing, dance, laugh, and cry.
This is your day, your someday: run, jump, and fly.

Be thunder in the sky, rain us with tears,
Bloom; pull free as clouds break and send us the light.
Give each of us a shadow to race through life
And bring dreams to the children every single night.

On Dream Horse, on Dream Horse, never stop
Oh Dream Horse, oh Dream Horse, never stop
On Dream Horse, oh Dream Horse, don't wait for me
Oh Dream Horse, on Dream Horse, always be free

The setting sun fills the world with jewels,
As bright stars on cloud-lips twinkle in the night.
And as all grows cold, these gems do harden,
Filling darkness with memories of the light .

50. Tempest

Cast me from your doorway
I ask this, my dear friend
Oh how your heart did stray
Be my stranger once again

~

O Rain, tap my fingertips
Recite your refrain
Play these ivory strips
Be a melody to pain

O Wind, lean 'pon my chest
My weight sustain
Caress this harrowed breast
Be a lover feign

O Cold, pull fierce the shout
From my lips so plain
Feel my warmth pushed out
Be a summer's shame

O Darkness, crack the sky
Of lightning entertain
To the wincing eye
Be a flawless curtain

O Grass, swirl at my feet
Make footing strain
Bind me like a bed sheet
Be the puppet slain

O Tongue, taste bitter dirt
My tear champagne
Off my chin came this dessert
Be feast for the brain

O Thunder, howl in my ear
Make the silence inane
Hush my objections here
Be a soloist's bane

O Papers, swirl from my hand
Spill ink from the vein
See dreams across the land
Be a poet in the rain

O Lungs, drown in the air
Let my sorrows rein
Choke away my prayer
Be the hoper's chain

O Heart, give thy beating
With your clinch restrain
To all these things fleeting
Be the windowpane

O Heaven
Bear witness to this sound
O Earth
Cry to your moon never found
O Love
To see the world gone insane
O God
To feel the tempest mundane

51. The Tear, the Sun, the Rain

I miss you
Like the tear misses the eye
Like the sun misses the morning dew
Like the rain misses the sky
I miss you

52. The Unwilting

Since no one knew me
Or set foot upon my stage
My death is merely melodrama
Filled with rage

You cannot cry
Because flowers die every day
Even if your sweet tears
Would help them (help me!) stay

53. For Me

I want you to be boring
Your beauty, the fire in your eyes
That smile, so full of life
It fills me, it thrills me
And I want those things to be mundane
I want to see such wonders every single day
I want you to be boring in the most splendid way

54. Candlelight

Like a flower before your lips
A budding chrysanthemum
The candle at your fingertips
Holds a light that is handsome

The glow, the laughter in your eye
More than a magnolia tree
More than the moon held in the sky
You, my love, inspire me

Puff! With a kiss blown towards the spark
A whisper
Becomes a question in the dark
My answer:

My wish? Is that what you want to know?
Closer, you move closer too
I should have said this long ago
Through the night, I reach for you

I can still sense you everywhere
And I wish, I pray only for this
That I will always feel you there
Forever in my darkness

"I love you"

55. The Surface of the Lake

Cold. It felt cold upon my face and I welcomed it.
The drops continued down my hot skin, tracing my
cheeks and chin like gentle fingers and put a cool scent
in my rabid lungs. A breeze I had not noticed before
took hold of my cold mask—pulled it softly from my
face—leaving room for the sun's unending kiss. Was I
blushing? Did the caress of this peaceful place put this
silly grin upon my face?

Just as before, I leaned forward and dragged the water to
my lips. Like love, fairies, or some other intangible thing:
water cannot stay in my fingertips. So I moved quickly,
drank quickly, and when it was all but gone, I tossed what
remained into my desperate face. Cold. Just as before.
What a wonder it is to live the same moment again.

Upon the third, I was stopped. My hands were gone,
cut perfectly at the wrists, beneath the surface of the
lake. My frantic play had stirred the shallow water,
and like all the monuments in heaven, it appeared
unnoticed: a cloud of mud. I tried to push it away, but
my actions only made it worse. A tempest in my hands;
a storm at my fingertips.

I could have left, but I waited. Lie: patience is always
a virtue. All I wanted was to experience it once more.
So I waited. Waited and stared at the surface of this
lake. Waited as the cold of the earth moved through
to my knees. Waited as the pain grew in the arch of
my back. But the moment came soon enough and the

water began to clear. And as it settled, long wisps of dirt flowed between my fingers like silk streamers, carried on the current of a liquid wind.

It was then that I noticed the reflection: the sight of distant birds and broken clouds fluttering overhead. It wavered ever so slightly, stirred by the drops that periodically fell from the sides of my face. The birds moved rapidly through the air, chasing the shafts of sunlight as they shifted between the clouds. Oh those clouds, they could not hold back the sun and let the light slip through their grasp, like water through fingertips.

I'd waited long enough and pulled my cupped hands from the surface of the lake. I paused. It wasn't cold. My hands had become acclimated to water. Worried, I tossed it in my face. It wasn't cold. I shivered.

It was then, as I stood, that I thought about the moments of my life. How many had I known like this? How many had I experienced before; how many would I experience again? Above all, how many would I never know again?

The chirps of birds rained down upon my head. I continued to blush as the sun winked through a shadow. One question remained. What was it that put this silly grin upon my face ?

56. Underneath Goodbye

How long will she hesitate at my door,
Trapped in that wooden frame there?
Forever, like a painting she is held,
An incomplete masterpiece, so fair.

Into the white canvas she is fading,
As snow clings to her coat and hair.
Nothing; she can find nothing to say,
Caught halfway between me and nowhere.

Over the horizon of her shoulder
Breaks the dawning of her eye.
I hear her, as she illuminates me.
Finally she says, finally, "Goodbye."

This? She hesitated so long for this?
What went unsaid and unheard?
What cowers, hidden in those twilight eyes?
What lives, what lies, beneath that single word?

The final painting has many layers,
Hidden chances and hidden shame.
What lost errors does the painter hide,
Trapped forever in a simple wooden frame?

How many melodies are sacrificed
In that final symphony?
How many snowflake miracles are lost
In that snowy landscape before me?

How many lines has this poet deleted?
How many words could I have said?
What thoughts in this heart and head somewhere lie,
Beneath my answer, underneath …

"Goodbye"

57. An Oak Tree Leans over a Country Road

An oak tree leans over a country road
And beneath it travel many a kind
In that ancient shadow they lose their own
But in that moment their lives intertwine

In summer they stroll through a field of stars
As a crown of leaves makes a patch of night
And through bejeweled gaps the sun falls
Filling that old shadow with points of light

In autumn visitors walk on water
As golden leaves fall from the branches' drape
Such raindrops disappear among their kind
Forming the surface of a sunset lake

In winter travelers receive angel wings
As gusts knock snow from boughs gone black
These pallid drifts form plumes about their heads
Tracing graceful arcs that settle with a flap

In spring the watcher see a renaissance
As they stand by a tree that's done aging
Yet with the sun stretching, on endless days
Once again that shadow is growing

An oak tree leans over a country road
And beneath it travel many a kind
All of them may someday be strangers
But in that shadow they leave something behind

"A good poem about love has never been written. It can't be done. Poems are about beauty and what can be more beautiful than love? It's impossible, but that doesn't mean it's not worth trying. No … poetry is about taking ordinary, mundane things and making them beautiful … What beauty could a poem lend to love?"

—*Walter Amber Wrights*

58. Something Impossible

Do you remember our walk in the field of rye
When the setting sun lingered in the ample sky
I don't know who forgot to reap them
In that very first day and hour of autumn
And left grains of gold to tickle your fair thigh

How, my love, did you know to stop then
At that exact moment, that percise second when
Walking a step behind you, I hesitated
Oh what beauty, your beauty, that awaited
Standing on a rise in a rye-covered glen

Your soft skin stole all the light the sun created
Oh what a shimmer that left the heavens sedated
Your hair took control of the wind's decree
And played conductor to a golden sea
Around you the world danced like a child elated

And as fate and chance and hope would have it be
You, my dear love, stole something else from me
Your beauty tore my body and very soul apart
And took what alone remained; you took my heart
Still, my love, never was something given so willingly

Oh how, my sweet, can a thing exist without soul or
body
How; how did you give something impossible to me

~

[<--- Ed. tear page away from binding]

Oh stop here, my love, and let this poem end
Please ignore that one unanswered question
Take my love and let it grow through the year
Know, my sweet, that every word was sincere
Do not ask why I hesitated then

Take this page and tear it here
Let that sound be my whisper on your ears
Let that touch be a tingle at your fingertips
Let that smell be my mouth upon your lips
Let the pieces flutter away like your fears

Let only memory of these words stay
Those feelings of doubt you must betray
But know the true beauty of this poem was you
And your willingness to do what you had to do
Please, tear this page and turn your doubt away

Carry the fragments as a sweet reminder
That it's only your sole beautiful I prefer
Tell me, tell me you don't need to know the end
Oh my love, let our love be like this poem
And say it's possible for a poem to last forever

Oh and if that isn't true—it cannot be—
Then please, please give something impossible to me

~

For if you go any further you will understand
Why I hesitated; why I am a tortured man
For in that sight I saw an angel I briefly knew
Yes dear, I loved someone else before I loved you
And I fear that it may happen yet again

Is love not enough so that I must betray you too
Oh what chance do I have if what I fear is true
What chance is there that you're not reading here
Is your love, all love, just as I've come to fear
Why, oh why couldn't you tear this in two

That's why you tore me to pieces so severe
Because only my heart was able to endure
But if a heart can survive, it can love anew
Is that why you kept reading on through
Is that why you stopped in the rye, my dear

Oh, did I hesitate or just stop quickly behind you
Could it be that you knew what you had to do
But why— You'll never have that chance, never
To tear this page and live with one love forever
Did you make this sacrifice for me, my love
Or did I sacrifice you

Is all love doomed to one day dull
Or is our love different,
Something truly impossible

59. A Nightlight Eulogy

Beneath a midsummer night sky
I watched a dim little light disappear.
To see a star suddenly die
Is indeed something rare.

No ash, no body, just panic,
No one to share this uncommon goodbye.
But who will dare to believe me?
Can Nothing be a lie?

No, this is a mistake of mine.
I've stared at the dark for far too long.
Slowly, I am becoming blind.
No, my star can't be gone.

Why was tonight peaceful and warm?
Damn you for making such a fragile speck.
Behold our tormentor's true form,
Heaven's failed architect.

It's just too dim to see it there.
I'll go and paint all the other stars black.
If you'll please just answer my prayer,
And bring my candle back.

Even now I forget its face.
God, tell me, was it blue or was it white?
I try to memorize its place,
In the dawning twilight.

All the markers are fading fast.
Your last sunset is a sunrise for me.
I was wrong; all the sky is ash,
And here is somebody.

--

Such a late star never heard many wishes
But somehow let it hear this eulogy:
I swear, until my own heart languishes
I'll carry your spark right here … with me

Nothing is a lie, my dear nightlight; goodbye

60. You Already Know

You already know how this will end …
Blinking, you greet the light of a sunrise,
Knowing the dark night will soon return.
Even the strongest flower someday dies.

Gently, he sets you on your messy bed.
You straighten the sheets as he climbs over.
Staying, he becomes your darkening sky,
His breath a summer breeze to savor.

You already know how this will end …
Like wind-chimes, you heard your mother's laughter
As you slowly walked to her funeral.
Even a flying bird must land somewhere.

Slowly, his fingertips explore your skin,
Like a blind man touching his missing son.
You wonder if he feels your soul shiver
As your jeans, blouse, and seconds are undone.

You already know how this will end …
In sixty years, your fingers grow too weak
To hold a brush and paint your masterpiece.
Someday, every song stops being unique.

His tongue belongs to someone else's lips,
Warm waves crashing lightly on his hard teeth.
Can he feel the torrent of your maelstrom
As he sips the nectar that lies beneath?

You already know how this will end …
Tonight will echo for the rest of time,
Even when you stand beside his gravestone.
The melting candle will not always shine.

As your bodies connect, he trembles.
Like violin strings, you shiver with him,
And what a song you make in harmony.
But what will come from this poem of skin?

The flowers he gets you will someday die.
The memories you make will slowly fade.
The horrors you regret will be common.
The passion will become mundane.

You already know …
You already know …
You already know …
You already know …

You already know how this will end …
Don't close your eyes when you jump off your cliffs.
You already know how this will end …
And you still love him, despite all of this?

If the answer is yes. You're a fool, my friend.
But being foolish never has to end

61. Dark of Destiny

The sacrifice of hiding in the light
Is not knowing where my darkness lies
And the shadow in the corner of my smile
Is just part of my utter disguise

      Let me out, let me out, says the fox to me
      Did you think Common was your destiny

Did you know. they spell tears and tears the same
Because tears mark the seams of men
But the beast, the beast, he never cries
Even if some days, I seem depleted

      Will you spy against humanity
      To be isolated but to be free

Oh reader, do you want to consume my lines
Do you feel jealous for some of them
Or fear or joy or awe or happiness
The proper emotion is boredom

      Because you fall for my disguise
      You never know where my darkness lies

Once broken, a bird's wing never soars as high
But don't let that fill you with sorrow or rage
It's rare to survive such an injury
Even if broken wings can only heal in a cage

      Let me out, let me out, says the fox to me
      Did you think Common was your destiny

62. The Artist

It's horrible.
How can it be so bad.
When the artist returns to his inspiration,
It does indeed turn out, Yesterday
He was mad.

63. An Unbroken Cup

The sky blue held in my palm is cracked
By the fake clouds left by flying jets
But this handheld heaven is intact
Because she fixed this cup of regrets

In life, so many hopes are broken
But like lies, the truth, and promises
Some dreams can be fixed or unspoken
While others stay a perpetual mess

A popped balloon differs from a bird
Whose wings can heal and someday fly
And while "Hello" is a truthful word
"Farewell" can easily be made a lie

While a rose bush cut will bloom again
And a kiss, once broke, you can renew
A fallen tree is at its end
Just like lost promises and smiles too

Like a teardrop, our moments shatter
But our memories, they never fade
Daybreaks are a permanent matter
But by those pieces our future's made

While hope lives and dies in moments,
Yesterday gets no renewal
And expectations always lament
While tomorrow has no funeral

So …

Break me, shake me, take me with an ax
See if I'm the unbreakable stuff
Every day, show me all of these cracks
So I may someday be strong enough

To hold our dreams and our fantasies
In a promise to never give up
And hold our world and our memories
In the space of an unbroken cup

64. Beneath the Linden Trees

It was an act of desperation. With the War coming to an end and Allied forces moving deep into the homeland, the Nazis deployed a special unit. This organized band of brainwashed children was aptly named the Hitler Youth. These young boys were given guns and ordered to protect pointless locations around Germany. In most villages, they were stripped of their weapons and sent home. However, this only brought down the wrath of the SS and led to the execution of village leaders and statesmen. In a dark and grim time, this act dimmed even the brightest of things: our hope for the future.

Can you hear them, hear them play
Here, where the linden branches sway
Can you see them dance, dance so tall
Above the ivy, on the cemetery wall

Their tepid flute makes a mellow song
To replace the songbirds that have gone

Oh Mommy, why won't you let me go
Oh Daddy, why won't you let me know
Of those other children playing there?
Besides, I didn't even like our mayor

Let me get back the cupboard for the hall
From the hangman's podium doomed to fall

Oh my child, oh my daughter, oh my son
What you ask simply cannot be done
Those aren't children beneath the sun
Those are soldiers, monsters with a gun

Oh what a misery, miserable as this
To see the play of children all amiss

Can you hear them, hear them play
Here, where the linden branches sway
Beneath the boots of the hanged
Here, where morality went insane—

Oh God, do not forgive us until we amend
Damn us who killed these children
And made them into men

65. A Snowflake (Born of Heaven)

In the dark, there came a glimmer
Whether an angel's wing or sigh of winter
Who knows what stirred our sky then
You were born of heaven

Like all those who came before you
Beneath a frigid sky of endless blue
With little or no choice at all
You began to fall

And while others rushed quickly past
Twisting, turning, and falling so very fast
Although this is why we're created
You hovered and you waited

Don't be afraid, little blossom,
Of when you finally reach the bottom
For you'll rest on the back and heads
Of family and friends

Oh look up, my dear snowflakes
And through those distant cloud breaks
See so many others coming to thee
See the stars that you set free

Oh you, you were born of heaven
And when you've finally melted
Flowers will grow up then
Marking beautiful that life you've led

66. Fence

How did I find paradise here,
Leaning against a wooden fence
In the shadows of a swaying tree
Surrounded by flower scents
Serenaded by the chirps of jays
With a loving pretense

On the gusts of warm wind
God brings the world to me
And hidden in a summer mist
The scents of a distant sea
By angels with butterfly wings
Hiding in the sunlight free

All the Truths are clearly written
In the clouds across the sky
Hidden behind the oak branches
They tickle my mind's eye
And fill me with memories
Of my life's many sweet lies

And as the soft skin of the earth
Drinks this soldier's essence
I briefly wonder what might lie
On the other side of this fence
But an answer is nothing with no question
And life is nothing without suspense

67. A Field Forever

Blades of grass are raindrops that never fall.
Their points, like fingertips, lightly tap your face
Before, back towards a sky so tall, they bend,
A thin archway for that magic place.

The wind is a whisper that never ends.
Its voice, like my soft voice, lingers in your ears
And in its pausing softly sends … a blush,
A light chill that soon disappears.

Summer sunsets are lovers who never rush.
Their warmth, like my warmth, runs so very deep,
And long into the night that hush is sealed,
A passion your heart closely keeps.

One day, someday, we'll lie in that open field
And spend our hours with the setting sun
Till the shadows dance with grass … gilded bright,
Those golden raindrops never done.

One night, some night, we'll kiss and pause often,
Using our loving hiatus to count the stars
And wishing on every light in the skies
That one more sweet kiss will be ours.

Our love is a meadow that'll never die.
Its life, like our own life, is truly boundless
And in its endless growing lies the truth
That this man, this soul, must confess:

In my youth, my day, and in my passing
My love for you is everlasting.

68. I Held Her

For such a brief time, I held a fairy
As she lay in my palm, weak and wary
Like trembling whiskers, her wings felt the wind
Like a falling star, she shone brightest then

Her eyelids were Romeo and Juliet
Two star-crossed lovers forced separate
For even in my fingers, as she rested
Her eyes, those gems, stayed slightly parted

"Why won't you trust me?" I said in whispers
Of the horrors my hidden tempest stirs
"I'd never hurt you, my little ember."
All demons and devils, but never her

Does the only truth in life come from death
Is the equation balanced like all the rest
See the horror and beauty, my friend
A story is nothing without her end

For never was a story of more woe
Than that of Juliet and her Romeo
Two lovers meet, her trust unopposed
Finally for me, her eyes softly closed

For such a brief time, I held a fairy
And heaven knows what I could not bury
My fingers burn from clawing at the earth
Now my weak grip forever knows its worth

If I could make a story without end
I'd write of that fairy forever, my friend

—Rin, I felt her life leaving

69. Since You've Been Gone

These days never end
And yet they seem so long
These days I've spent with you
Since you've been gone

One empty chair at a table meant for two
I sit with my shadow and thoughts of you

These dreams never end
Someday they'll come true
These dreams you told to me
I've kept them for you

One spontaneous laugh without your echo
Is a lonely silence that I've come to know

This love never ends
And so I let them go by
A second chance at love
My second chance to live and die

On a park bench where we stared at stars above
My seconds are lost in the hour of our love

These lies never end
The heart has no memory
So I fill our promise
With fantasy

This isn't a fairy tale or tragedy
This is a story without end

Romeo and Juliet meet only once
Hamlet never dies
The Prince kisses her
But never sees the fluttering of her eyes

The lion dances with the tiger
The wishes stop at two
The hero saves us
But never comes home to you

This hope never ends
And so it is a lie
I could end it if I had the courage
To say … "Goodbye"

And all those promises and all those dreams
I've kept safe for you
As I wait for you
Since you've been gone

Oh, this isn't a fairy tale or tragedy,
This is a poem without end
And you and I shall write it forever … and ever again

[movie version]

70. Iron Foxes
(a self-portrait)

Where the setting sun makes rusted wheat shine
And the dancing wind and rolling hills collide
In a retired field, the iron foxes play
Racing their shadows through an endless day

Metal scarecrows caught in a single stride
Whose fading coats turn red with stoic pride
So far away, they seem more than fantasy
And that's why he stopped our journey

It was a mistake; he thought they were real
And yet Clarity is hard to conceal
So he blushed and whole world blushed with him
As the lowly clouds turned bright and crimson

With eyes held tight, he slowly turned to me
The wind, his hair, the wheat all dancing free
"I'm sorry," he said and somehow smiled
"The first fox I ever saw in the wilde"

"Go." I whispered soft. "Run." And he listened
"Escape that cage, fly, and be unreason."
With arms held high, he quickly ran from me
What folly, he lived in that fantasy

Such a place, where humans somehow fly
Where the heroes come home and never die
Where dragons talk and life lives in the stars
Could such a world ever truly be ours

Where the setting sun makes rusted wheat shine
And the dancing wind and rolling hills collide
In a retired field, the iron foxes play
Racing a young boy thru an endless day

It was a mistake … I thought it was real
For a moment, this was all I could feel
My skin tingling cold at warm summer winds
Such wonder, to live in this world of his

It was a mistake, a beautiful mistake, it seems,
To love hope and be the dreamer dreaming

71. Notes and Asides

Nigh is almost night. The price of love is an eternity.
To the trees that fell to make these pages: I repeat the
whispers of your memory. "For me ..." appears fourteen
times in this book. You cannot stop counting, you
soldier with eyes of blue. Look—be a poet in the rain—
see shadows silhouette reality. It's a secret the flowers
know, this is what I do, crowd the world: a quarter
century. Earth, sun, death, sky, life—I stole. There is a
secret hidden in my heart, like a second in an hour. The
sunlight slips; the world is my conspirator. If there is a
star lost in the light of the moon, then it is me. And I
still shine bright. The oak tree never pines for winter. If
there is love lost in the light of your smile, then it is me.
And I still love her. "Sorry, Sping was not found in this
dictionary." What but the mind of an educated man has
the power ... to contain madness in a teacup and an
eternity in an hour? Where the crow and his dear, dear
petal flew (the kiss lasted a lifetime—the lifetime of a
kiss) beneath a sky of blue. Everything fades, waiting
for my surrender. I was a villain when I left you, over
the horizon of her shoulder breaks the dawning of her
eye. The moment becomes merely a second. The scents
of a forest drenched in rain. He made love to her like a
candle to its flame: melting around her with tears on his
face, burning long into the night until he was spent and
darkness came. Never's coming. Oh, this isn't a fairy
tale or tragedy; this is a poem without end. She dances
in the field, twisting and turning like a sparrow falling.
As she dips low, towards the earth, her hands snap out,
touching the tips of the winded wheat. The wings are

spreading. She flies once again. I reach for her, I watch her … Fly. Carry me to heaven. Be wilde. My love fills the promise of an empty door. That sounds wonderful. Can I go there? A life lived is a life worth living. Open the window. I love you.

Synopses of Longer Works

A Fox Dream – A Novel
Completed: 2007

Synopsis: He lost. The great, undefeated warrior lost, and as he fell into the arms of the poet, he made his confession. He lost on purpose. Now his title and his responsibilities belong to his killer, an artist named Arachi Senda.

Arachi won't have long to recover from his duel, as the new Koto-Kai will soon be needed. Murder has invaded the Hidden Kingdom, a forbidden place on the far side of the empire. Only the most privileged diplomats are allowed to visit the sacred location, and if Arachi isn't careful, he might send the empire back to war. Fortunately, our poet is not alone. As he tries to solve the murder and unravel the mysteries of the Hidden Kingdom, he is guided and protected by his best friend, a female samurai named Tatami.

The poems in this book are written by Arachi, the protagonist, and Princess Eyoe, the girl trapped inside the beautiful prison called the Hidden Kingdom.

Related Poems: 5, 6, 27, 28, 33

The Prince of Tears – A Novel
Completed 2004

Synopsis: After the assassination of his parents, Prince
Setter is forced to take over the burdens of a dying
kingdom. He'll do whatever it takes to save his people.
He'll fight a dragon, take over the world, and fall in love
with a cat. He'll give his mind over to a wizard, become
a hero, learn to play the lute, and die a villain. This is an
epic story of love, sacrifice, and redemption. This is the
story of the Prince of Tears.

The poems appearing in this book are written by Kendra,
a girl gifted with the ability to control dreams, and Rayn,
a vagabond duelist who rises to challenge a king.

Related Poems: 7, 8, 10, 29

~

Since You Been Gone – A Screenplay
Completed 2006

Synopsis: A million dollars. The offer seems too good
to be true. Lyon Wilde was an unknown poet until the
day he saved a stranger from suicide. Along with a six-
story drop off a bridge, Lyon's heroics brought him fame
and success, but it isn't just the media that's taken an
interest. He's also caught the attention of a devil.

Now, a year later, the poet is contacted by eccentric
billionaire Richard Ramshold. He offers Lyon a million

dollars for a single poem. No strings, no stipulations. Lyon accepts the money, and that's when his world changes. Fame and fortune begin to take their toll on the man's simple life. The poet becomes less important than the poem. The woman he loves becomes less important than the woman he saved. The fairy tale becomes less important than the tragedy.

Related Poems: 23, 31, 63, 69

The dreams never end . . .

www.KitsuneDreams.com

Back Cover Image by: Cassandra Bruynseels
Front Cover Design by: Elaine Ward
Help by: Paul Hawley

Thank you for making my dreams real ^_^